CW01662244

For Kajsa, T

www.samsarabooks.com
www.siebposthuma.com
www.kajsablomberg.nl

© 2023 text Jan Paul Schutten
© 2023 illustrations Sieb Posthuma
© all illustrations heirs of Sieb Posthuma
© 2023 English translation Brendan Monaghan
© 2023 This edition, Samsara Books, Amsterdam

Agency Kajsa Blomberg Amsterdam
Design steef liefting
ISBN 978 94 93301 70 2
NUR 400

No part of this publication may be reproduced without the express and written permission from Uitgeverij Samsara / Samsara Publishers, Amsterdam.

Amsterdam Stories

Sieb Posthuma &
Jan Paul Schutten

Samsara

Waterdivers

A city full of canals is beautiful but also dangerous. The Amsterdam Fire Brigade has to rescue dozens of people from the water every year. That this mostly involves people who fall in while peeing is a myth. The victims are usually fully clothed – with their fly done up. They are almost without exception men. And because emergency services aren't always needed, the actual number of people who fall in the drink is probably considerably higher. This means that someone falls into the water almost every day in the summer. On average, eighteen people drown in the canals each year, in half of the cases, under the influence of drugs or alcohol.

Whatever the number of people who end up in the canals, it will never be as bad as December 31, 1790. The combination of a holiday and extremely thick fog claimed many lives that evening. Some sources say about forty people ended up in the water and "remained dead" in a single evening. For the "rattle guards," tasked among other things with getting people out of the water, there was no end to their work. Publicans weren't only hard at work drawing beer but also looking after those lucky enough to be saved. They were obliged to – those who didn't do so, risked a fine.

In those days, first responders used various methods to revive victims, including bloodletting, ammonia salts, brandy or simply vigorous rubbing. The barber surgeon Mozes Zadok had the strangest method for bringing people round: he used bellows to pump tobacco smoke through the patient's anus. But Zadok was a seasoned professional, saving a total of 26 people.

When it comes to experience in saving people, Dirk Rietveldt is the champion. Most people don't even know his surname because he was chiefly known as Dirk the Water Diver or Uncle Dirk. He was famous in the Jordaan for having rescued 74 people from the canals. As well as dogs, cats, bicycles and even cheeses. This figure isn't a meticulously kept record but Dirk's own estimate. He regularly bumped into people who told him that they owed him their life. "I dive into the water as someone else would swat a fly away from their nose. Splash! Right in," in the hero's words. Official police reports only credit Dirk with fishing ten people out of the water. A respectable number, nonetheless.

Rescuing people was lucrative. For each person Dirk saved from the water he received three guilders from the police. Sometimes even more from the family. A cat once even fetched him fifteen guilders from the animal protection society. A large sum for Dirk, who mostly earned a living as a porter or bridge-hauler – someone who helped lift heavy carts over a bridge. Occasionally he supplemented his income by filching goods. He was arrested for stealing six cauliflowers and a dustbin (and twelve times for public drunkenness). Apart from money, Dirk was regularly awarded medals for his heroic deeds, and was decorated by no less than three Dutch monarchs. When he wasn't nominated, he put himself forward. Eventually he was given a hero's pension of five guilders. Not bad for a descendant of Dutch naval hero Michiel de Ruyter. Well... according to Dirk again, who was originally from De Ruyter's birthplace, Vlissingen.

As people like Dirk are thin on the ground these days, the city has had to take other measures to prevent drownings. This is why several handholds have been placed in the canal walls, which people who have fallen into the water can hold onto. And in recent years the municipality has installed ladders so that people unfortunate enough to fall into the drink can clamber out. No decrease in incidents has been reported so far; there are more than ever before. Not just the number of victims but also all the shared-use scooters that end up in the water and are mistaken for bodies.

Playing the field

Even though adultery is as old as humankind, it still fascinates us immensely. Countless entertainment shows, gossip magazines, novels, soap operas and of course "juice channels" rely on it for their popularity. However, we have come to view it differently over time. For centuries infidelity was illegal and subject to stiff punishments. Those who were rich enough usually got away scot-free, but if you were poor – or even worse, female – you weren't so lucky. Women weren't only punished more severely but more often too. Penalties ranged from hefty fines to public humiliation, imprisonment in the rasp house, the spinning house or even banishment.

In 1774, Jan van der Tuuk discovered that the consequences of infidelity could also be dramatic for men. The Amsterdam draper had smuggled his lover (dressed as a young Englishman) as discreetly as possible into his home but was caught anyway. His wife, Anna Carolina de Wit, immediately invoked their "carnal conversation" as a reason to divorce him. But this wasn't the end of the story: carefully crafted pamphlets with poems and a caricature appeared shortly after the incident. The drawing showed Van der Tuuk fleeing in a nightgown with a night cap on, while his lover still lay half-naked in bed. There was also a sizable delegation of law-enforcement officers in the room. The pamphlets were highly effective. Even years after the incident, many Amsterdammers wouldn't be seen in public with Van der Tuuk.

Extramarital relationships were an offence for an exceptionally long time in Dutch law. Yet many people openly admitted committing adultery, even if they hadn't. This is because infidelity was one of the few legitimate grounds for divorce, until the law was revised in 1971. Most of the people who did so were men, as women lost their right to alimony if they confessed to an affair.

Admitting infidelity could be an attractive strategy for other reasons, as attested by a weaver in the Anjeliersstraat, at the beginning of the eighteenth century. The man from the Jordaan rowed so often with his wife that they ended up living separately, at which point he committed adultery. As the marital squabbles continued, often exacerbated by drunkenness, they were regularly hauled in front of the church council. Eventually, they were even punished and placed under supervision. Their names: Jan Klaassen and Katrijn Pieters. Historian Jan ter Gouw says it is no coincidence that they share their names with the Dutch equivalent to Punch and Judy. He found the tale of the duo in records dating from 1706. According to Ter Gouw, Jan Klaassen later mended his ways and quit his job at the weaving mill to become a puppeteer, earning him far more money. Their many quarrels and shouting matches must have been an ideal source of inspiration for the marionettes' adventures.

Amsterdammertjes

Amsterdam is built on piles. Yet however essential these piles may be, a completely different kind of pole has become the symbol of the city. What could be more typical of Amsterdam than the painted iron bollards called amsterdammertjes? And to think that they almost disappeared from the streets. If the municipality had had its way at the turn of the century, they would have been removed one by one. It wanted the city to be emptier, more spacious and above all less cluttered. This clutter was partly the result of an earlier decision by the municipality. Whereas the original bollards weighed at least seventy kilos, the cheaper sheet-steel models, in use after 1972, weighed less than a third of this. These lighter bollards were much easier for lorries to knock over, resulting in thousands of crooked bollards.

Not everyone agreed with the decision to remove the amsterdammertjes because it also meant the loss of over two-hundred years of history. As early as the eighteenth century, similar posts were used as bollards to protect houses against the iron bands on cartwheels. Later they were also used to shut off roads and bridges, such as the Melkmeisjesbrug, which has the oldest bollards in the city. These last look slightly different to current models, having changed colour since 1915: from dark to white to maroon. According to tradition, the first amsterdammertje was a cannon barrel still containing a ball, and the shape of later bollards was based on this model. This isn’t such an outlandish idea if you consider their present shape. But the first bollards didn’t look at all like a cannon. They were slimmer and stood on a square base, so the cannon story can’t be correct.

The municipality’s policy initially led to a rapid reduction in amsterdammertjes, from about 100,000 in 1984, to just under 38,000 in 2003. Yet the enthusiasm with which they were removed eventually vanished faster than the bollards themselves. Maintaining order in the city starts with the attitude of Amsterdammers and when the bollards were removed, more and more city dwellers began parking their cars unlawfully to “load and unload goods.” It made more sense to park your car incorrectly than to park without paying. As it had become impossible to enforce parking policy, most of the bollards have been put back in recent years. Otherwise, we would have had to go to Leiden, Ghent or Leuven to see amsterdammertjes.

Megalomania

Compared to nearby capitals, Amsterdam has a relatively modest architectural style. Amsterdam isn't a city for bombastic buildings, the palace on Dam Square being the sole exception. Joost van den Vondel even called the building the "eighth wonder of the world." In terms of size, it still pales in comparison to the Royal Palace in Madrid, the Louvre in Paris or the Victor Emmanuel II Monument in Rome, but it doesn't fall far short of these buildings in its delusions of grandeur.

The megalomania is visible from Dam Square. Architect Jacob van Campen designed what was the world's largest secular building in his time. A grand total of 13,659 piles were needed to support the 22,000-square-metre edifice. And all of this for a town hall, not a royal or presidential palace. This is how important Amsterdam considered itself in 1648, the year construction started. The grandeur took on even greater proportions inside. The floor of the Citizen's Hall, for example, is adorned with the largest maps in the world, made by Amsterdam top cartographer, Joan Blaeu. Two maps depict Earth's eastern and western hemispheres, and a third one shows the night sky.

Amsterdam is the centre of the universe in these maps. And with ships from the city sailing to all four corners of the world, this wasn't even such a strange idea. Discovering the world often started in the Dutch capital. The Dutch East India Company and

XXX

the Dutch West India Company even had their own cartographic services. A commercial spirit and science went hand in hand. For the best atlases in the world, you also had to come to Amsterdam. And especially to Joan Blaeu. For instance, he created an atlas 1.80 metres tall and one metre wide, intended for King Charles II of England, as well as the renowned Atlas Maior with six hundred maps.

On the roof of the palace is a completely different Atlas. This mythological Titan took on Zeus, was defeated and his punishment was to hold up the heavens on his shoulders. Artus Quellinus' six-metre-tall statue has been standing for centuries, exposed to the elements, with his gaze directed down towards the Nieuwezijds Voorburgwal. The beautiful view of the city must be his only comfort. If you want to get a better look at Atlas, you don't necessarily have to go onto the roof. The casting model of the statue is in the Citizen's Hall, so it can be admired from close up. Besides, this version is in far better condition than the weathered colossus outside, which has endured countless tempests and hailstorms.

Atlas used to regularly receive a distinguished visitor. Queen Wilhelmina liked sitting near him on the palace roof to paint, enjoying the silence and the panorama. As an amateur painter, she worked on several pieces there. The statue of the Titan was a favourite subject of her paintings. Doubtless, she felt some affinity to him: lonely but not alone, burdened with an immense weight on her shoulders.

Legend has it that Amsterdam will be lost when Atlas drops the heavens. Unlikely as it is that the whole city would be endangered if this thousand-kilogramme copper sphere crashed to the ground, however a substantial crater would be formed in the pavement, at the very least. Fortunately, the statue is closely monitored from its left and right by Justice and Prudence, and occasionally by the Cultural Heritage Agency as well.

Rembrandt

Damage

A dog *Night Watch*. Well, why not? There is a version with Dutch celebrities. There are photos with lookalikes or with essential service workers. There is one with figures from the Dutch amusement park, Efteling and there is a Duck Watch. There are Lego and Playmobil-themed editions, jigsaw-puzzles and versions made from various materials – embroideries and mosaics made of flowers, aluminium plates and wooden clogs. Living "Night Watches" can be booked for parties and events. In short, the numerous versions range from successful art to well-intentioned handicraft. This is all a bit much for some people, but they should bear in mind that the painting itself has endured considerably harsher treatment.

The worst damage occurred in 1715. The artwork was moved from its original location in the Kloveniersdoelen to the Small Court Martial Room in City Hall (now the palace on Dam Square). It didn't fit nicely between the doors, so four strips were lopped off, the biggest on the left side. A total of about 2.3 square metres of the work were permanently lost. Luckily, Frans Banninck Cocq had commissioned the painter Gerrit Lundens to make a small copy of the original, giving us a rough idea of how it had looked – even more beautiful!

In the complete work the two main figures, Banninck Cocq and Van Ruytenburch, were depicted farther to the right, so they appeared to lead the troops. In its current state, the painting is much more static, and they seem to stand still. The Rijksmuseum exhibited the work in its original form in 2021. A reconstruction of the missing sections was made using Lundens' painting and artificial intelligence. The exhibition of the complete work was such a success that there was much talk of permanently displaying the Night Watch in its entirety. But Lundens was no Rembrandt, so it is a matter of speculation how the two militia guards on the missing portion were actually portrayed. For the sake of authenticity, the museum decided to stick with the smaller version for now.

Happily, other damage had less serious consequences. A seaman attacked the canvas with a butcher's knife in 1911. He had been declared unfit for service and wanted revenge on the state. The painting came off relatively lightly on this occasion. But someone slashed it again in 1975, with much severer consequences. A man suffering from mental illness cut an entire strip off the Night Watch and the restoration took more than eight months. In the period between these two attacks, the painting also endured a great deal during the second world war. To prevent it being plundered by the Germans, the painting was hoisted out of the museum and then, rolled around a cylinder. It ended up in a safe near the Castricum dunes, before finally being stashed in Mount Saint Peter near Maastricht. The most recent attack on the painting was in 1990.

An attack on the Night Watch is an attack on the country, which explains why no painting has been attacked more often than this masterpiece. For this reason, it is the only painting with its own unique escape route. Shortly after Hitler came to power, a slot was made for the painting so it could be lowered through the floor of the museum in one go. Anyone walking through the cycle tunnel beneath the museum can see it. If a fire, terrorist attack or any other disaster occurs in the museum, it is "women, children and the *Night Watch* first".

Riots

It can't be denied that the history of Amsterdam is also one of riots. Just think of the squatters' riots that started about half a century ago. Or how often the Leidseplein has been vandalised by hooligans when Ajax won the championship. And, of course, rioting opera goers! As in Amsterdam you could find firebrands in all walks of life, so in 1761, a group of elegantly wigged noblemen caused an uproar in the theatre because they felt cheated. The city's upper crust created such a commotion that not only was the performance cancelled but the disturbance persisted for months.

It was all about a performance by the stunning Italian diva, Anna Davia. Or rather, the lack of a performance by the singer. Anna Davia had come to Amsterdam half a year earlier to be the star of Domenico d'Amicis' company. But befitting a true diva, she behaved as might be expected. She clashed with the group's leader over all manner of things, especially money. D'Amicis eventually replaced the singer with his daughter, Anna Lucia, who sang at least as admirably. In fact, she deeply impressed even Mozart. But the audience hadn't come for Anna Lucia. They hadn't even come for the opera. They had come for Anna Davia and d'Amicis hadn't said she was being replaced. "Boo, boo, boo – go away and bring on Davia!" they chanted with no sense of metre or rhyme.

Even in the posh Amsterdam opera, emotions could run high. It isn't so surprising as opera was popular in the city, even if the

Netherlands has had little to contribute when it comes to opera composition. The Germans had *The Magic Flute*, the Italians La Traviata and the French *Carmen*. The Dutch had to make do with Johannes van Bree's Saffo, with a libretto by Jacob van Lennep. Written in 1834, the piece was based on the Greek poet Sappho. The name was expressly changed because everyone kept pronouncing it "Sap-ho" during rehearsals. The five-hour-long piece was described as one of the greatest triumphs in Dutch art. The performance did indeed draw full houses and was showered with prolonged applause, but it soon faded into obscurity. Revivals have been staged every once in a while, only for the work to return to the dusty archives soon afterwards. Amsterdam opera productions have been an international sensation in recent years, but often still based on foreign classics.

Since the 1980s, opera performances in Amsterdam have been associated mostly with the white building on the Waterlooplein that everyone calls the "Stopera." But its architect, Cees Dam, never uses this name. He always speaks of City Hall and the Opera because the other name has such painful memories. For you would be wrong in thinking Stopera was a combination of the Dutch words, Stadhuis and Opera, rather it combines *"stop"* and *"opera."* The fact that residential buildings and a large part of the Waterlooplein were sacrificed to build the enormous theatre and city hall caused major riots when construction started in 1982. Squatters, hooligans and perhaps even the odd opera goer doubtless took part.

Canals

A painting without paint. A lawn without grass. A bicycle without wheels. This is Amsterdam without its ring of canals. And to think that the heart of Amsterdam very nearly came to resemble a place like Lelystad, with lots of parking, wide thoroughfares and far more office space in the city centre. While Rotterdam was destroyed by the Germans during the war, Amsterdammers nearly did the same thing to their own city a few years later. It was all down to a plan by Chief of Police, Hendrik Kaasjager.

In 1954, Mayor Arnold d'Ailly ordered Kaasjager to improve the traffic and parking situation in the city. He immediately set to work, soon concluding that the canals had more or less lost their practical function. This represented much untapped potential. The Singel could be closed. As well as the entire Singelgracht, in fact. And filling in the Lijnbaansgracht, Kloveniersburgwal and Geldersekade would give you a nice broad thoroughfare, with plenty of parking. D'Ailly posed a question and Kaasjager supplied a proper answer. It probably wouldn't have gone any further than this review if a journalist from the Algemeen Dagblad hadn't got wind of the proposal.

Disclosing the plans naturally provoked howls of outrage, but they also received a surprising amount of support. Why should Amsterdam be a large open-air museum when it could also be a modern business city? Besides, many buildings had been seriously

neglected; so why shouldn't the winds of architectural change blow through the city? Why shouldn't a motorway go straight through the city? And while on the subject, when the Kloveniersburgwal and Geldersekade are filled in then the Waag and the Schreierstoren will have to go too as they block everything. And the palace on Dam Square for that matter.

Publicly airing such opinions was one thing, but the biggest problem was that the opinions belonged to influential people. Modernisation of the city drew nearer and nearer. Matters were made worse by the poor condition of many buildings and the continued deterioration of the city. It was better to have sturdy, modern office buildings than historic ruins on the verge of collapse. Quite a few people thought this made sense.

For many Amsterdammers, it was time to sound the alarm. The "Maatschappij tot Stadsherstel" (Society for City Restoration) was established two years later. Its main goal was to protect the old city from generalised urban planning. The "De Stad Amsterdam" committee was set up to discuss traffic issues. Traffic had to adapt to the city, not the other way around. And together with organisations like the "Vereeniging Hendrick de Keyser," various historical buildings were purchased to protect them from demolition and modernisation.

The Weesperstraat and the Wibautstraat could no longer be saved. Historical buildings were demolished here and there because of their architecture, which many people considered completely out of place in their current environment, such as the University Library on the Singel and De Nederlandsche Bank on the Frederiksplein. But eventually it was possible to keep enough streets intact until the storm of modernisation abated. Some argued that Kaasjager deserved a medal for waking up the city with his plan. In any case, it confirmed a famous Amsterdam philosopher's (i.e. Johan Cruyff) proposition: "Every disadvantage has its advantage."

Pigeons

It all started in the Middle Ages when poultry traders bred rock doves to sell at market. Their descendants evolved into domestic pigeons, and these urban pigeons went on to conquer Amsterdam's squares, streets and roofs. A local church was named after them. A Dutch pop song was made about them. And they pose every day with hundreds of tourists visiting the city. If one bird symbolises Amsterdam, it is the pigeon. Despite some people calling them "flying rats," nowadays there are about 15,000 pigeons in the city. There were many more in the past. And many less at times.

It isn't surprising that rock doves, of all birds, have been so successful in cities. The animals are easy to fatten up, which made them extremely popular with the poultry buyers' guild centuries ago. But the birds' natural habitat plays a role too. The shape and colour of building facades resemble the cliffs and mountainous regions they originated in. Moreover, roofs are ideal places on which to build safe nests. The animals' excellent navigation abilities made them extremely suitable as carrier pigeons, further increasing their popularity among pigeon fanciers. It was almost their undoing in the second world war because it made the Germans want to get rid of them.

A special police unit was formed to exterminate the pigeon population within a few weeks of the occupation of Amsterdam, in May 1940. The Germans were terrified that local pigeon fanciers would

ZOUT

use the animals to send messages from the Dutch resistance to England. The Pigeon Brigade introduced a decree forbidding the "release of pigeons of any kind to fly freely" as early as June 1940. Anyone who caught a feral pigeon could collect a reward from the police. All pigeons in dovecotes had to be registered, which in the first two years of the war, amounted to some 32,709 birds. Eventually, pigeon keeping was completely forbidden, and people ignoring this order risked execution.

This decree meant that all pigeons in Amsterdam were to be destroyed forthwith. All pigeon fanciers had to do this themselves and hand in the severed, ringed feet to the police, as proof. This was asking for trouble because no one wanted to kill their prize pigeons. Favourite pigeons were taken into hiding, while less fortunate birds were given their leg rings. Feral pigeons were also supposed to be exterminated, but this didn't go smoothly either. The Pigeon Brigade, which meticulously monitored all pigeon flights, still recorded around 200 pigeon flights on some days.

However hard the Germans tried Amsterdam's pigeons were never wiped out. In fact, after the war their population rose rapidly and now there are many thousands of them again. Central station alone is home to about 125 of the birds. But fifty years after the pop song about pigeons in Dam Square was written, it is still the place you will find by far the most pigeons.

Peace and quiet

Once upon a time, if you were looking for peace and quiet in Amsterdam, you could find a corner in a park that almost no one knew about, or a courtyard no one visited. With the growing hustle and bustle in the city, this corner would have to be an even more obscure park or courtyard. Or perhaps a remote corner of the Amsterdamse Bos or another "green zone" outside the ring road. Space and quiet were becoming more and more difficult to find. But fervent skaters and cyclists knew of an alternative. They had long ago discovered a haven of peace and quiet, just above Amsterdam North.

Once you have passed beneath the electricity pylons, you find yourself in a stretch of countryside containing picturesque villages with wooden houses clustered around a church. Holysloot, Durgerdam, Ransdorp and Zunderdorp, places with their own history and often considerably older than Amsterdam. These villages are skirted by lakes and canals, which are even more idyllic when there has been a cold snap. Surrounded by meadows filled with bearded tits, reed warblers, bluethroats, bitterns and other birds which make a birdwatcher's heart flutter, they are all just a few minutes' bike ride from the city. This haven is also an officially designated quiet area. Or quiet area 33 to be more precise. The idea is that the sounds of flora and fauna can be heard above noise. And sometimes this is indeed the case.

At least… when there aren't any vintage-car or motorcycle rallies with dozens of participants passing through. When Schiphol Airport hasn't decided that all jets may fly as low as they can over the area. When there aren't any hunters, even before the break of dawn defending the fields of perennial rye grass from ducks, hares, geese and other threats. When delivery lorries and vans stick to the speed limit. When the wind blows the sound of the party boats in the other direction. When there aren't any traffic jams nearby, tempting cars to use the narrow roads as a shortcut.

And then indeed it sometimes can be quiet there, if only for a moment.

Mazel Tov

Quick-witted, brimming with humour and always in for a joke or a stunt, you couldn't find a more typical Amsterdammer than businessman Loe Lap. His jovial character made him more than just a well-known Amsterdammer but a Dutch celebrity in the 1960s and 1970s. His qualities were recognised in Hilversum, the Netherlands' TV capital, where he was always ready to give his unvarnished opinion, both on radio and TV, whatever the topic. Luminaries such as Mies Bouwman, Willem Duys, Sonja Barend and Ischa Meijer liked to invite him regularly onto their shows. And he was an excellent presenter too. None other than Johan Cruyff asked him to be the master of ceremonies at his wedding. Loe's dog was also well known in the city. It let itself out every day – not going from tree to tree, but from butcher to butcher.

Above all, Loe Lap was known for his surplus store in the upscale Reguliersbreestraat, opposite the jeweller Kan. The jeweller's slogan was: "Wat Kan kan, kan Kan alleen" (What Kan can do, only Kan can do"). Lap decided to advertise with "Wat Lap lapt, lapt Lap alleen" (What Lap pulls off, only Lap pulls off). When the shop opened, Johnny Kraaijkamp and Rijk de Gooyer rowed down the street in a boat, much to the delight of the gathered crowd and the annoyance of everyone travelling the same route by car or tram. Anyone could come to the store to find unwanted army supplies

and related merchandise, varying from parachutes ("If it doesn't open, just bring it back") to mine detectors and transistor radios ("Now with a built-in swimming costume!")

Partly thanks to its humorous advertising, Lap's surplus store was a great success. He even created national trends. Tens of thousands of secondary-school pupils had army packs as school bags in the 1970s, or they wore Afghan coats like the ones Lap sold in his shop. But his greatest successes were jeep antennas used as radio receivers, periscopes which served as binoculars and affordable walkie-talkies. He bought everything in massive quantities and sold them for a song, a new concept at the time. And a method that wasn't always appreciated by colleagues at the posher shops in the street. His bargain-basement products contrasted starkly with the luxury items in nearby stores.

He never knew what would sell well, he just knew that something would sell well. "Ten-percent mazel tov is worth more than ninety-percent skill," Lap reckoned. He wasn't always in the shop, but when he was, he would yell across the shop like a market trader, "Yes, folks, everyone is getting a good deal today." He preferred doing business at the bar or the coffee shop around the corner. On the occasions when he was in his office, he was usually lounging on his chair, with his shoes on the desk, talking on the phone. His talent wasn't hard work but "schmoozing." This is also how his career took off. "Without spending a single cent on capital outlay," he managed to create a big business with his smart talk.

Lap began his career just after the second world war, when he had to do everything just to make ends meet. He would go to Central Station with an empty suitcase and strike up a conversation with traders on their way to sell their goods. By "sheer chance" he said he was heading for the same place with exactly the same goods. He proposed taking some of his colleague's stock and selling it somewhere else. Then they wouldn't have to compete and could share the proceeds at the end of the day. This ruse earned him enough to start trading for himself later. He wasn't afraid that things would go wrong. This was because of the war. "They murdered my whole family. What else could happen to me now?"

However funny and jovial Lap was, the war always played an enormous role in his life. His parents died in Sobibor and his brother in Auschwitz. Loe and his sister survived by hiding for years. He had had so little exercise that after the liberation of Amsterdam, he even had to learn to walk again, with the help of his future wife. Every other sorrow paled in comparison to his wartime grief. Therefore, he was rather stoical when his empire of surplus stores went bankrupt. As long as he could still go to the Rembrandtplein with friends to discuss events in the world and laugh. Above all to laugh.

Stripping off

The world of prostitution is a murky world of human trafficking, exploitation and modern slavery. And it always has been. While some still write wistfully about the times when the atmosphere in the Wallen was more friendly, even this period was rife with threats, violence and murder. The romantic image of how the Red-Light District was a few decades ago is mainly thanks to the stories of the leading lights in this world, such as Haring Arie, Blonde Mien and the Fokkens ladies. They were shot to fame by the documentary, *Ouwehoeren* (Old Whores) and of course, Appie Baantjer's popular detective novels.

The bar for nicknames wasn't set all that high in those days and once you had earned a nickname, you could never shake it off. Haring Arie Elpert earned his nickname by selling herring (haring) on the Rembrandtplein for a short time in the 1950s. Parijse Leen got her name from having been to Paris once. Chinese Annie was as Dutch as windmills and clogs but had dark hair. Kapstok Jantje (Hatstand Jantje) had broad shoulders and a narrow head, while Blonde Mien, Wil de Paardekop (Wil the Horse's Head) and Magere Josje (Thin Josje) are pretty self-explanatory. Zwarte Jan (Black Jan) was an exception, who managed to ditch his nickname. By his own account, his wife made him go grey, after which he was called Jan de Bollebakker (Jan the Bun Baker).

I L O V E
Y O U

These nicknames also reveal how some practices in the sex industry have stayed the same, even though the words for them have changed. Mooie Henkie (Handsome Henkie) and Mooie Willem (Handsome Willem) seduced and manipulated their girls into working in the industry for them. In about 2000, the euphemistic label "lover boys" was adopted in Dutch for men of this kind. The term sounded so positive that people soon wanted rid of it. The Minister of Justice unsuccessfully proposed replacing it with the Dutch equivalent of "teen pimp." In Flanders, the word *pooierboy* (pimp boy) has come into general use. But pimps didn't always have the final say. Local legend has it that Blonde Mien had her husband and pimp Haring Arie under her thumb, just as she dominated many other men. No one understood the art of "earning" like she did.

The idea was to make as much as possible with as little effort as possible. And this involved stripping off your clothes, both for the woman and the customer. Every item of clothing removed cost money. As did every additional service. For the woman, the ideal situation was for the customer to leave as soon as possible, without having sexual intercourse, with his wallet far lighter and yet satisfied. A premature climax was not unwelcome either. Then she would say, "Oh, what a shame. Better luck next time. Come back soon." The women from back then regard their successors with dismay. They are dressed far too skimpily, leaving little for them to "earn."

Solution

Amsterdam has struggled for centuries with whether or not to tolerate prostitution. And when tolerance wasn't the problem, it was where the women plied their trade. Plans to remove the windows and brothels in the Wallen are more serious than ever these days. But where would the prostitutes go? The municipality has proposed three places, already provoking significant protests. However, there is also another solution, allowing the Red- Light District to keep its current function without exploitation and without disturbance...

Although the situation was quite different in the city's early days, there is a certain logic attaching to the association of Amsterdam's oldest neighbourhood with "the world's oldest profession.". When Amsterdam started expanding rapidly after obtaining city rights in 1342, wealthy residents lived in the houses between the protective walled canals. But over time the city's growth and increasing wealth caused them to move to larger houses in the canal ring. The neighbourhood became a place where craftsmen, dockworkers, sailors and prostitutes lived.

Much has changed over the years, but prostitution has never completely disappeared from the Wallen. Centuries ago, its brothels already drew people from outside Amsterdam to the city. Prostitutes were sometimes tolerated for a time and then banned again

IN DE VERGULDE PEENIS

KAMER TE HUUR

but they never went away completely, not even in the prudish nineteenth century. The area started to deteriorate around 1900, and the Red-Light District eventually became a free zone for everything that was prohibited: gambling, taking opium, paid sex. The neighbourhood's popularity reached its zenith in the 1960s. Amsterdam was known as the most tolerant city in the world, and the Red-Light District drew hundreds of foreign and local visitors every day.

Its popularity made Amsterdam a magnet for hardened criminals from around the world. This resulted in a sharp increase in human trafficking and the sale of hard drugs in the 1970s. However, visitors to the Wallen faced little danger thanks to the old guard. It used a couple of tricks to maintain order. If someone was robbed near Casa Rosso, owner Zwarte Joop would offer a huge reward to track down the wrongdoer. Joop made up the description himself, which was immediately circulated everywhere. Joop wasn't interested in catching the thief; he wanted everyone to know that they should leave his customers alone. This is why the Oudezijds Achterburgwal was even called "the safest street in the world."

Nevertheless, the atmosphere became grimmer, and the neighbourhood deteriorated to such an extent, even the tourists stayed away. Residents found the municipality's policy much too lax and protested against the decline. The municipality responded with various measures. The area was improved, illegal brothels were closed, and the police patrolled day and night. Then the volume of tourists increased as never before, which wasn't good for the neighbourhood either. Complaints about drunk visitors, public urination, bachelor parties in penis costumes and vomiting coffee shop visitors even reached the rest of the city. And why must the most beautiful streets in Amsterdam attract the most dissolute tourists? Visitors who also spent little and steered clear of museums and cultural attractions.

The municipality eventually responded with a plan to relocate the erotic business out of the city centre. Two suitable locations were identified in the vicinity of the RAI, in the well-heeled "South," and another option was in "North" near the NDSM wharf. Publication of the plans provoked several protests by people living or working nearby and they haven't been implemented so far. But Sieb Posthuma came up with a brilliant solution years ago: put men in the windows. Gigolos! It would make the Wallen unique again and less attractive to public urinators, drug tourists and boozers. Bring it on, Blonde Rien, Chinese Henk and Willem de Paardekop...

View

In the 1990s, Amsterdam broadcaster AT5 featured an item on what most struck foreign tourists about Amsterdam and its residents. Apart from the Wallen and the coffeeshops, tourists were surprised by the carpets on tables in cafés, food that you could get out of lockers in a wall and the cyclists you could see everywhere. Even people in smart suits cycled to work! Tourists also thought it strange that such tall people lived in such small houses. Speaking of which, you could easily look into many of these homes. You saw exactly how they lived, what they were doing and which TV programme they were watching.

Amsterdam had also been a source of surprise centuries earlier. Various seventeenth-century diaries and travel journals mainly contained complaints about the city's stench. Couldn't they flush those stinky canals a little more often? Another striking observation was how freely Dutch people brought up their children. Jan Steen's paintings, in which children get up to all sorts of things, was excellent proof of this. They might have been an exaggeration of reality, but such scenes were unthinkable in paintings by old masters from other countries. And children in Amsterdam were brought up even more freely than in Jan Steen's hometown, Leiden. Sometimes foreign visitors wrote with horror about how children behaved here. Which has, incidentally, always remained so. This horror can still be seen on the faces of foreigners in restaurants watching in silence how parents let their children run around between the tables, screaming.

Recently a bureau that supports expats in Amsterdam conducted research among foreigners in the Dutch capital. Carpets were no longer mentioned, and neither were respondents surprised by Febo vending machines. They seemed accustomed to the bicycles, but not yet to the sheer number of cyclists, who also spurned helmets. And certainly not to their anarchic cycling behaviour, paying no heed to red lights, directions and other rules. Many non-Europeans also found it bizarre that you have to pay for public toilets. Restaurants still took some getting used to – now because of the staff's rudeness. Other peculiar customs were King's Day, New Year's Eve, children being allowed to light fireworks, and even doing so as early as November, was completely unthinkable in their home countries.

As well as surprise at children's and cyclists' behaviour, they were still amazed by Amsterdam's residential architecture: the stairs were dangerously steep and the rooms too small. Again, they mentioned the lack of curtains in windows. In Belgium, roll-down shutters are lowered at the end of the afternoon – if they have been raised in the first place. In mediterranean countries, shutters prevent other people from seeing what is going on inside the home. In most other places, curtains are simply drawn, while in Amsterdam… not only is everything allowed, but you can see everything too.

Freedom

History repeats itself but never in the same way. Centuries ago, freedom of religion caused an influx of traders and other influential people who helped make the city great. Hundreds of years later, freedom in areas like prostitution, drugs and sexual morals put the city back on the international map. This happened in a remarkably short period, with little sign in the early 1960s of the pioneering role Amsterdam would come to play in tolerance. In the end, it only took two years and a handful of people to set a change in motion that would still be felt decades later. It is questionable whether Amsterdam ever could have become what it is today without the provo movement.

Amsterdam already had the Cobra art movement, the Vijftigers in literature and the nozem youth subculture, so a basis for cultural change existed. But in many ways, Amsterdam was still a very conventional city. The first truly successful anarchist actions started with the provo movement in 1965: smoking marijuana in public, the happenings of anti-tobacco magician Robert Jasper Grootveld and comical demonstrations – such as walking around with empty placards and handing out raisins. Such actions were provoking and confusing to the establishment and all of them were provo.

The movement encountered considerable resistance in the beginning but because provo made people laugh and advocated non-violent demonstrations, its reputation and support grew, and

it gained attention. Newspapers that at first had ignored its activities started writing more and more about it This was also because there were violent campaigns at the time which made international news, such as letting off a smoke bomb at the wedding of Princess Beatrix and Prince Claus. Provo wasn't responsible but benefited from the worldwide media interest these events attracted.

The provos also attracted increased attention because of their sympathetic ideas. Like Luud Schimmelpennink's White Bicycle Plan: bicycles painted white and free for everyone to use. This was followed by the White Chimney Plan which proposed a stricter policy against air pollution. The White Woman Plan sought to end the taboo on sex and public education on birth control. The White Chicken Plan wanted the police (the "chickens") to engage in more social work and the White Housing Plan, which was a protest aimed at real estate investors speculating with vacant properties when there was a housing shortage; this subsequently became the blueprint for the squatters' movement. Regardless of your opinion, it was impossible to see harm in any of it.

Provo's meteoric success led to its rapid demise. The movement certainly wasn't supposed to go mainstream, so it disbanded in May 1967. According to one of its founders, Rob Stolk, provo wasn't even meant to be a movement but an idea. Roel van Duijn and other early participants later founded the Gnome Movement, but this initiative had an even shorter lifespan than provo. Still, the fire provo had lit continued to burn.

The tourist office reported increasing numbers of camping tourists and people wanting to know where to buy marijuana. And slowly but surely various provo symbols found their way onto Amsterdam tourist brochures. The city's freedom proved to be an important selling point. "The Dutch have stopped being dull," a British journalist wrote at the time.

Thanks to the city's new image, freedom in one area fostered freedom in another area. Amsterdam wasn't only the city of red lights and coffee shops but of gay bars and discos. The world's first gay wedding was in Amsterdam and nowhere did the squatters' movement grow as large as in Amsterdam. But the most important kind of freedom was a mentality. Whether you roller-skated through the city wearing just a thong or paraded as a drag queen through the Kalverstraat, whoever you were or whatever you wore, you could do anything in Amsterdam.

Slowly but surely, these freedoms have crumbled bit by bit. Perhaps one day Amsterdam will even lose its liberal image. It remains to be seen in which area the city will play a pioneering role again. Hopefully, we won't have to wait as long as last time.

Hippies

Sometimes people fight for freedom, sometimes about freedom. Amsterdam might have a very tolerant image, but the transition to a city with such free morals didn't happen without a fight, literally. Princess Beatrix knew all about it. Not only was her wedding day marked by violence, but squatters organised violent riots at her coronation, with the slogan, *"Geen woning, geen kroning"* (No house, no coronation). Earlier, in 1959, the "nozems" had been clubbed on Dam square – their attackers included Haring Arie and Zwarte Joop. In 1970, the same place was once again the scene of violence; this time the hippies' turn. Dozens of "Dam sleepers," young tourists who slept on Dam Square, either because they couldn't find or couldn't pay for somewhere to sleep, were heavy-handedly set upon by marines.

Fortunately, Amsterdam had somewhere else that was much more tolerant and where everything was allowed, the Vondelpark. A year later, in 1971, every hippie knew where they had to go. Around the ponds, on the grass between the trees in the park, there were hundreds of sleeping bags by June, mostly occupied by bearded men and a few girls – almost with flowers in their hair. It was clear that the Vondelpark was going to be the world's hippie Valhalla that summer. Everyone was excited. People played guitars and sang songs, smoked marijuana and protested against the war in Vietnam. Love, peace and happiness.

The municipality provided baggage storage, toilets and washing facilities. The cost of the entire "Vondelpark project" was, according to some estimates, as much as half a million guilders. This included subsidies for healthcare workers, such as nurses and field workers, who provided information on responsible drug use. It was no bad thing as around eighty percent of the tourists were on narcotics: half used cannabis, a third used other substances like LSD, and a tenth used hard drugs like heroin. This immediately led to another significant expense, emergency medical care and hospital admissions. The "summer of love" was thus transformed into the "winter of discontent," and what the hippies thought would be paradise turned into a mecca for dealers of marijuana and other drugs.

As time went by, the young hippies were joined by more and more less well-intentioned youth, such as petty criminals from France and Italy. Eventually, a fifth of the people in the park consisted of some variety of criminal. Hundreds of young people were robbed, mugged or swindled by "dealers" who fobbed them off with all sorts of rubbish supposed to be hashish or hard drugs. Not to mention the drug dealers who came to Amsterdam. Dealers could already be found around the Wallen, the Warmoesstraat and the Nieuwmarkt district, but events in the Vondelpark strengthened the image of the city as a place where everything was allowed. Making matters worse, the summery weather gave way to prolonged bouts of rain, making the Vondelbrug the only place in the park where you could sleep and keep dry. The deteriorating weather immediately caused the atmosphere to deteriorate, resulting in more and more fighting and violence. Eventually, the hippies disappeared from Amsterdam, but the dealers stayed on.

Bicycle city

"Just look at them." "The things they come up with these days." "They're show-offs. The lot of them." "I recently saw three of them in the Leidsestraat!" Reactions to the first cyclists in Amsterdam would have been something along these lines. A century and a half ago, bicycles were still extremely expensive and exclusive, but gradually they became more affordable and grew in popularity. Especially in Amsterdam which, apart from Copenhagen, was later voted the best bicycle city in the world. Its ascent to the top of the ranks wasn't without obstacles, both literally and figuratively. If there were a top ten list of obstacles in Amsterdam, parked bicycles would undoubtedly occupy first place by a wide margin.

The fact that Amsterdam has become the domain of cyclists is due to a combination of policy, luck and lucky policy. Fred Feddes and Marjolein de Lange conducted research into the reasons for Amsterdam's success as a bicycle city and concluded that the city offered ideal opportunities. It is a happy coincidence for cyclists that Amsterdam, as the Netherlands' capital, hasn't been the residence of the head of state since Louis Napoleon. Palaces and government centres require broad avenues and boulevards, which subsequently proved very suitable for conversion into motorways. Amsterdam never had any broad avenues or boulevards. Likewise, the canal ring made the efficient flow of car traffic impossible. The size of the city also contributed to the success of bicycles because regardless of where you lived, you never had to cycle long to get to

the centre. And this was thanks to plans that worked better than intended.

Amsterdam drafted an ambitious expansion plan when, a century ago, the city began to expand massively. The idea was that new districts, such as Buitenveldert and what is now Nieuw-West, would have plenty of light, air and space. More accessible than older neighbourhoods, but not excessively so. In this new vision, the city centre and the major industrial and harbour areas should be reachable within a half-hour bike ride. This wasn't driven by ideological considerations but a pragmatic goal, as bicycles were the primary mode of transportation at the time. The plans were still being prepared when the war broke out, so they were only implemented in the 1950s and 1960s. Just in time, as cars were going from strength to strength. These districts were already finished by the time cars overtook bicycles as the most popular mode of transport.

However, cars had become unstoppable. They weren't only the most comfortable way to reach your destination, they were also a status symbol. Their popularity grew so fast that the municipality was constantly on the back foot. Authorities were more than willing to give cars plenty of space, but they simply didn't manage to do so effectively. With all the new wheels hitting the road, the city grew more and more congested and polluted, so much so, that counter movements began to emerge. So many car accidents occurred in 1970 that 114 people died in Amsterdam alone. This led to the advocacy group, "Stop the Child Murder" being set up, followed by the Amsterdam Cyclist's Union a few years later. Various protest events were organised, including thousands of cyclists on the Museumplein. Eventually, the municipality realised that bicycles should be given ample space, not cars.

These days bicycles are the most popular mode of transport in the city. Amsterdammers cycle more than two-million kilometres a year and this number is growing steadily. The municipality initiated a major plan to further cater to cyclists in 2017. Maps adorned with "green carpets," "royal routes" and an enormous expansion of bicycle parking facilities. The avenues and boulevards that Amsterdam never had, have indeed been built, but for cyclists instead. To crown it all, serious plans now exist for a long-cherished dream: a bridge for cyclists over the IJ has been talked about since 1839. It is still a long way off, but it is increasingly likely that cyclists will one day no longer have to cross from north to south and vice versa on a cold, windy ferry.

Terminal

It is in the way, cost tens of millions of euros, is more polluting than thousands of cars, is disruptive and has given Amsterdam city council enormous headaches for years. But it is quite something: the Passenger Terminal, the mooring area where millions of cruise passengers make their first acquaintance with the city every year. These numbers have made Amsterdam one of the most important cruise ports in Europe for decades, which is extremely lucrative. Docking fees, supplies and passenger spending easily generate several hundred thousand euros of revenue per ship. Little wonder the Amsterdam port authority opened a brand-new cruise-ship terminal at a prime spot on Piet Heinkade in 2000. However, it immediately unleashed a storm of criticism.

Amsterdammers have become increasingly annoyed by the increase in tourists in recent years and cruise passengers are no exception. They don't walk through the streets with noisy wheeled suitcases at six in the morning, they don't stumble around the Red-Light District or leave half-empty bottles of cheap alcohol and pizza boxes in parks, but when a ship full of tourists disgorges its passengers, they cause a sudden peak in the hustle and bustle of the city. And it isn't as if they spend that much money during their short stay ashore. Besides, the ships cause at least as many problems as their passengers.

Northwest Territories
NEW YORK

CHIGAGO
RIO
Fort Mc Murray
Silverton

The biggest problem is that the ships use bunker oil, a kind of black lava filled with chemicals and heavy metals. Fifty cruise ships running on this oil emit more sulphur dioxide than all 260 million cars in Europe! This is disastrous for the climate and the city. In addition, almost two thirds of nitrogen pollution in Amsterdam comes from these ships. The municipality has responded by compelling shipping companies to use electricity from the power grid. All ships will use this facility by 2025, decreasing pollution significantly, but it will still be enormous.

And on top of this, the ships hamper all sorts of ambitious projects. *The Splendida*, a gigantic block of flats 333 metres long and 58 metres tall, docked at the terminal in May 2015. Even if Amsterdam were to allow ships only half as tall as the *Splendida*, bridges over the IJ would still have to be at least thirty metres above the water. This leaves only one option: relocate the mooring area. The existing terminal will have to go, and a new one built elsewhere. Completely forbidding cruises is for now, still mission impossible…

Bridges

Amsterdam consists of hundreds of little islands through which the Amstel and the canals meander. Consequently, the city has more than 6500 bridges. But which of them is the most beautiful? Most people would immediately think of the Magere Brug, or "Skinny Bridge," because this one bridge symbolises the "real" Amsterdam. The Magere Brug was built at the end of the seventeenth century and was at first extremely narrow, so probably where it gets its name. Its original nickname was the "Kippetjesbrug," or "Chick Bridge," as "kippetje" was colloquial for a thin girl in those days: you could only walk over it if you were very skinny. Later, the bridge was widened greatly, even wide enough for car traffic. Its current iconic design only dates back to 1934 but fits seamlessly with the architectural style of the city's most glorious century.

The Magere Brug probably wouldn't have been considered the most beautiful bridge in the 1950s. The Utrechtsebrug, a structure that is hardly noticed these days – and certainly not for its beauty, was called the most expensive, largest and most beautiful bridge in Amsterdam. In 1954, tens of thousands of people cheered at the opening ceremony of this new connection over the Amstel and for a week afterwards, the neighbourhood celebrated the new 250-metre-long grey hulk that brought you straight into the Rivierenbuurt.

In addition to the Magere Brug, the Scharrebiersluis (Scharrebier Sluice) is sometimes mentioned, a kind of oversized bridge that looks like it is made of Meccano. The bridge dates back to the nineteenth century but its current form is from 1906. Aficionados of the architectural style of the Amsterdam School often choose the P.L. Kramerbrug on the Amstel, designed in 1919. Then there is of course the Blauwbrug, inspired by the Pont Neuf in Paris. For many Amsterdammers this bridge is too pompous for the city. The Amstel isn't the Seine and Amsterdam isn't Paris, they argue.

The Koekjesbrug (Cookie Bridge) has been a good candidate since 2007. Columnist Martin Bril wrote an ode to the structure in that year, and it has appeared everywhere since then. The bridge likely owes its popularity mainly to its name because, architecturally, it isn't particularly unique. There are various explanations for the origin of the name. The most logical explanation is that there were several chocolate factories and a cocoa mill in Oud-West. Chocolate was sold as "cookies" at the time. And these "cookies" probably travelled over this bridge into the city centre.

In 1971, director Guy Hamilton had to choose from all these bridges for a backdrop scene in *Diamonds are Forever*, starring Sean Connery. Of course, he chose the Magere Brug. James Bond cycling over the Koekjesbrug really would have taken the biscuit. Many years later the bridge appeared in another film, this time Dick Maas' *Amsterdamned*. The film actually features dozens of bridges during a long chase scene. Maas knew the city like the back of his hand and exactly where to take the most spectacular shots of Amsterdam: above the Amstel, on the Singel and on the Oudegracht in... Utrecht. This is because Amsterdam doesn't have any low terraces on its canals, unlike its smaller neighbour.

Elite

For as long as the canal ring has existed, it has been the place Amsterdammers most want to live. The most expensive and sought-after homes have always been between the Prinsengracht, Keizersgracht, Herengracht and the Singel. These houses have been inhabited by people with money and status for so long, that throughout the Netherlands the canal ring has become synonymous with the haughty elite. But does this image really hold true? The Ambassade Hotel, located in the "Negen Straatjes" (Nine Streets) area on the Herengracht and the Singel, investigated who the past residents of the ten plots in the complex were. This illustrates nicely which professions the wealthiest people had throughout the centuries.

The Herengracht was originally called the "Eerste gracht," or "First Canal," but was soon given its current name because of its rich-gentlemen (heren) inhabitants. Anyone with a large amount of money lived there. Companies were barred from the canal until 1850 because manufacturing, storing or processing products was often accompanied by a foul smell, which gentlemen weren't exactly keen on. The Singel was the first moat around the city, dug in 1428. It might be "de Singel" in Dutch, but it is "het Singel" in Amsterdam, and Amsterdam linguistic rules overrule official Dutch rules. Well... only in Amsterdam.

ZOETWAREN

Early residents of the buildings along the Herengracht and the Singel usually had professions that we wouldn't immediately associate with great wealth today. They included a mason, a skipper on a cargo-handling barge, several carpenters, shoemakers, tailors, hatters, furniture makers and even poets, with Jan Tengnagel being the most famous. The other half consisted of residents you would expect in Amsterdam high society, such as (grain) traders, nobility, an apothecary and a regent of the Maagdenhuis girls' orphanage. The professions changed in the early nineteenth century. Bankers, merchants and especially lawyers and notaries replaced older crafts. There was still one mason, Johan Hendrik Knuf, the well-known bookseller Frederik Muller, as well as various artists, including Reinier Craeyvanger, musicians and (master) carpenters.

Notable residents included politician Ferdinand Domela Nieuwenhuis, who was born there, and Anna Staringh, who worked as a magnetiser and hypnotherapist for the Amsterdam beau monde around 1900. The prices of these properties have risen so astronomically since the turn of the twenty-first century that they are increasingly used as offices for large pension funds, publishers and the like. The most famous resident in the previous century was without a doubt Simon Vestdijk, who produced such an extensive body of work that it was said he could write faster than God could read. The Ambassade Hotel bought its first buildings in 1953, and it has expanded over the decades like a cultured diamond. The hotel hasn't forgotten the history of the many writers, poets and artists, later even being known as a writers' hotel. Not only because it has hosted numerous international literary grandees, but also because of its extensive library with over five thousand signed books.

Its connection to the art world has remained at least as close, causing a great stir when a large painting was discovered in the hotel. The management was convinced it must be an exceptional piece.

An early Flemish master? Brueghel the Elder or the Younger? Or perhaps one of their pupils? It could easily have been so, considering the number of art dealers to have visited the hotel. They didn't have to wait long for a professional opinion as the expert on old masters at Sotheby's was a regular guest. His initial expression when viewing the artwork revealed little, but his subsequent verdict was clear: "It's nothing. Totally nothing." But this didn't deter the hotel from investing in art. It now has a collection of 800 works by members of the Cobra art movement, which are... genuine.

BRONNEN

Waterdivers
NRC, Martin Kuiper, March 25, 2017
Het Parool, Marius van Melle en Maarten Hell, December 29, 2019
Ons Amsterdam, Marte van Santen, June 28, 2007
Stadsarchief Amsterdam, April 23, 2019

Playing the field
Jan Klaassen Museum
Amsterdam City Archives, April 23, 2019
Vereniging voor Gendergeschiedenis, Timo van Barneveld
Misdadige vrouwen, Manon van der Heijden
Andere Tijden: De echtscheidingswet van 1971
Gescheurde bedden: oplossingen voor gestrande huwelijken, Dini Helmers, 2002

Amsterdammertjes
Ons Amsterdam, Emma Los, June 2004
Het Parool, Marc Kruyswijk, May 13, 2016
Amsterdam.nl, Ulli Fischer, September 26, 2005

Megalomania
De Groene Amsterdammer, Koen Kleijn, August 2019
Amsterdam-Monumentenstad.nl, Alice Taatgen, June 2019

Damage
Trouw, Flip van Doorn, December 2017
Andere tijden, April 2017
IsGeschiedenis
Rijksmuseum, June 2021

Riots
Trouw, Henny de Lange, September 2011
Ons Amsterdam, Maarten Hell en Marius van Melle, March 2021
De Groene Amsterdammer, Piet Gerbrandy, January 2000

Canals
Amsterdam.nl, September 2021
Ons Amsterdam, Peter-Paul de Baar, July 2006
Bijlmermuseum.com, September 2015

Pigeons
Amsterdam.nl, April 2019
Thedutchhistorian.nl, Axel Stam, December 2021
Amsterdam City Archives, April 2019

Mazel Tov
Ons Amsterdam, Carolus van Doornen, June 2011
Trouw, Afra Botman en Eric Brasem, April 1993
Joodsamsterdam.nl, April 2016

Stripping off
De wallen in de jaren '60, Raoul Serrée, 2015
Hoge bomen in de misdaad, Zwarte Joop de Vries, March 2006
Panorama, Pim Christiaans en Bas van Hout, November 2017

Solution
Hoge bomen in de misdaad, Zwarte Joop de Vries, March 2006
NPO Kennis, "Hoort prostitutie op de Wallen niet gewoon bij de Amsterdamse cultuur?," 2023
Amsterdam City Council, "Results of location study Erotic Centre," March 2023

CREDITS

View
eXpat eXperts, 2022
Geschiedenis Magazine, Kees van Strien, August 2019

Freedom
De Groene Amsterdammer, Marcel ten Hooven, july 2021
Ons Amsterdam, M. Schmidt, November 2011
DUB, Rinze Benedictus, June 2003

Hippies
"Heroïne en de stad", Gemma Blok, 2016
"Geschiedenis van de Nederlandse drugsbestrijding (1961-2011)," Jack Wever, June 2020
Ons Amsterdam, Marius van Melle en Niels Wisman, March 2012

Bicycle city
Amsterdam City Council: "For Cyclists a Healthy and Accessible City," 2017
Fietsstad Amsterdam, Fred Feddes and Marjolein de Lange, 2019

Terminal
Het Parool, David Hielkema en Tim Wagemakers, November 2022
AD, Erik Kouwenhoven, June 2019

Bridges
Onh.nl, June 2016
Trouw, Haro Hielkema en Hans Marijnissen, September 1995
Feitjes.Amsterdam, February 2022

These illustrations have been previously published:

Flyleaves of *De leeuw is los!*, Annie M.G. Schmidt, Querido, 2006

P. 18 illustration in *De leeuw is los!*, Annie M.G. Schmidt, Querido 2006

P. 21 *Rintje (Rembrandt)*, column Sieb Posthuma, *NRC Handelsblad*

P. 59 illustration in *Mannetje Jas*, Sieb Posthuma, Querido 2006

P. 70/71 illustration in *Het Grote Rintje Voorleesboek*, Sieb Posthuma, Querido 2011

P. 55 *Vrijheid*, set design *De Uilenpriesters van Orplid*, play by Christianne Stotijn

With thanks to Querido.
Other illustrations have appeared in articles and columns in newspapers and magazines.